Blue Beard

Emma Rice

methuen | drama

LONDON • NEW YORK • OXFORD • NEW DELHI • SYDNEY

METHUEN DRAMA
Bloomsbury Publishing Plc
50 Bedford Square, London, WC1B 3DP, UK
1385 Broadway, New York, NY 10018, USA
29 Earlsfort Terrace, Dublin 2, Ireland

BLOOMSBURY, METHUEN DRAMA and the Methuen
Drama logo are trademarks of Bloomsbury Publishing Plc

First published in Great Britain 2024

A catalogue record for this book is available from the British Library.

Library of Congress Control Number: 2024930399

ISBN: PB: 978-1-3504-7648-6
ePDF: 978-1-3504-7649-3
eBook: 978-1-3504-7650-9

Series: Modern Plays

Typeset by Mark Heslington Ltd, Scarborough, North Yorkshire

To find out more about our authors and books visit
www.bloomsbury.com and sign up for our newsletters.

Blue Beard: A Wise Children, Birmingham Rep, HOME Manchester, Royal Lyceum Theatre Edinburgh and York Theatre Royal co-production. First presented in England at Bath Theatre Royal on 2 February 2024.

Writer and Director	**Emma Rice**
Composer	**Stu Barker**
Set & Costume Designer	**Vicki Mortimer**
Sound & Video Designer	**Simon Baker**
Lighting Designer	**Malcolm Rippeth**
Movement Director & Choreographer	**Etta Murfitt**
Music Supervisor & Arranger	**Ian Ross**
Fight Director	**Maisie Carter**
Music Director	**Stephanie Hockley**
Associate Director	**Laura Keefe**
School for Wise Children Trainee Director	**Tom Fox**
Costume Supervisor	**Lucy Martin**
Wigs, Hair & Make-up Supervisor	**Fay Lumsdale**
Props Supervisor	**Charlotte Neville**
Casting	**Wise Children**
Producer	**Monica Bakir**

Cast

Lost Sister	**Mirabelle Gremaud**
Trouble	**Stephanie Hockley**
Treasure	**Patrycja Kujawska**
Lost Brother	**Adam Mirsky**
Mother Superior	**Katy Owen**
Lucky	**Robyn Sinclair**
Blue Beard	**Tristan Sturrock**
Sister Susie of the Dulcimer	**Stu Barker**

Production

Production Manager	**Cath Bates**
Company Stage Manager	**Anne-Marie Williams**

Deputy Stage Manager	**Kate Foster**
Assistant Stage Manager	**Madeleine Herbert**
Head of Sound	**Charlie Simpson**
Sound No. 2	**Harriet Hollinshead-Lee**
Head of Wardrobe	**Brooke Bowden**
Wardrobe No. 2	**Chloe Moore &**
	Maisie Higgins
Lighting Programmer	**Victoria Brennan**
Relighter & Production	
Electrician	**Laurence Russell**
Costume Maker	**Kirsti Reid**
Knitting	**Amanda Martin &**
	Emily Kingston Lee
Costume Alterations	**Jackie Young**
Props Makers	**Ernesto Ruiz, Smart**
	Models & Sarah Crispin
Production & Rehearsal	
Photography	**Steve Tanner**

With thanks

Sam Jones, Siobhán Harper – Ryan, Emma Tompkins, Alistair Turner, Matthew Hellyer, Nandi Bhebhe, Samuel Blenkin, Isabel Adomakoh Young, Chichester Festival Theatre, Helen Hall, Kate Stubbs, Akila Cristiano, Jamie Misselbrook, Paul Kieve, Emily Saner, Gemma at My Boutique Stay, Phil Hurley at Stage Sound Services, Silk Mill Studios, Setaway Transport and the Wise Children Club.

This production was made possible by the generous support of Cockayne Grants for the Arts – a donor advised fund held at The London Community Foundation – The Golsoncott Foundation, The Garrick Charitable Trust, the Theatre Artists Fund and everyone who gave to Wise Children's Big Give Christmas Challenge 2022.

We are delighted to have received a significant donation from Emma Rose, on behalf of her late father Courtenay Young, both of whom are great lovers of theatre. The show must go on.

Wise Children

Wise Children is a theatre company created and led by multi-award-winning director, Emma Rice. Founded in 2018 we are an Arts Council England National Portfolio organisation. From our home in Somerset, we make ground-breaking work with exceptional artists and tour across the UK and internationally.

Our home, The Lucky Chance, is in Frome, Somerset. Originally a 1900s Methodist Church, last year we transformed The Lucky Chance into our creation space and a tiny theatre in which to welcome audiences of all shapes and sizes. The Lucky Chance opened to the public for the very first time in December 2023 with Emma Rice's production of *The Little Matchgirl and Happier Tales*.

The School

Alongside our shows, we run a unique professional development programme, The School for Wise Children, training a new and more diverse generation of theatre practitioners. Led by Emma and her award-winning collaborators, The School for Wise Children offers workshops, courses and other opportunities for fearless, free-thinking theatre makers and emerging companies. For more information about The School and how to train with Wise Children, head to our website: www.wisechildren.co.uk

The Club

The Wise Children Club is our community: a growing group of allies who support our work and share ideas and dreams. Right now, as we face uncertain and difficult times, we need the Club more than ever! Club members are our ambassadors – online and in-person. They spread the word, bring new people to our shows, and look for opportunities for Wise Children to grow as a creative force for good! You might also be inspired to know that everyone who works for

Wise Children (from those who tread the boards to the Board itself) joins the Club and donates to the company. If you'd like to join us, you can do it at www.wisechildren.co.uk.

Foreword by Emma Rice
Artistic Director of Wise Children

I never liked *Blue Beard* as a story. It gave me the creeps and I avoided it. I thought it was a strange morality tale that bolstered the fantasy of dead women and taught us to allow men their secrets . . . sod that, I thought!

Then, a couple of years ago, the story started to tap on my shoulder and nag at my edges. Perhaps it was about more than I had first assumed?

Haunted by the regular chime of real-life women being attacked, murdered and abused, something started to click. I needed to tell this story – not to understand Blue Beard, but to breathe life into the women he tried to control. I needed to express the rage, grief and heartbreak so many of us experience and yet feel powerless to change. At this point in history, Sarah Everard had been murdered, and the ensuing chaos of her vigil had captured the public's imagination. However, for me, it was the murder of Zara Aleena that really brought home my anger and my loss. She was just walking home. A week later her family, friends and people she would never know, met at the spot where she was killed and walked her memory home. In silence. I cannot even write about this without weeping. This was the moment that I knew I wanted to walk Blue Beard's victims home. I wanted to use my craft, my platform and my experience to make a small difference.

It's been a long creative journey to create this multi-layered and complex piece. Supported by my company and key collaborators, we have workshopped ideas with care and caution. What has emerged feels palpably raw, relevant and powerful. The room laughs, sings and dances as always – but there are also tears. Tears we don't try to cover or apologise for. Tears that need to be shed.

As a community of theatre makers from all ethnicities, backgrounds and genders, we stand together to tell this story. We hold hands and hearts and with a collective cry we say:

Enough is enough.

Perhaps Wise Children is growing up.

Blue Beard

'For my dear and much missed dad – the original good man.'

Prologue

We are outside a convent.

Several **Sisters** *are going about their unusual business. They wear long smocks, headscarves and whistles round their necks. They are playing cards and smoking pipes, playing ball and reading the paper.*

One looks at her watch and blows her whistle.

On this signal, the **Sisters** *extinguish their pipes and put down their sporting equipment. They come into position for the daily service.*

Mother Superior *enters. She is small, scary and sports a bright blue beard.*

Mother Superior   Welcome to the convent of the Three Fs!

Sisters   Amen

The **Sisters** *do not make the sign of the cross but make another gesture more fitting to their mental state. It is more drill than genuflect.*

Mother Superior   At ease.

The **Sisters** *relax.*

Sisters, we have some parish notices before we begin the Daily Service:

The key to the firearms cabinet has gone missing . . . again.

It's a large gold key and it's attached to a keyring that says 'I've ridden the Worm at Chessington World of Adventures'.

So, all keep your eyes peeled for them please.

Sister Constance from Lost Property has been in touch to say there have been two new finds this week.

One – A stab-proof vest size XXL.

And another, a signed photograph of Fatima Whitbread so any takers for those, let Sister Constance know. Lastly, let's end the parish notices on a high. Our Senior Choir of Sisters will be performing their a capella version of Ricky Martin's 'She Bangs' this evening. That's at 7.45 in the Jiu Jitsu Suite. Let's show our support and give them a nice full house.

Without further ado, let us commence our Daily Service.

There is a collective breath in, but before another word can be uttered, a young man appears in the auditorium.

Lost Brother   Hello!

*The **Sisters** spring to action and square up to him.*

Lost Brother   Hello?

The young man wears a sad rucksack and has an even sadder soul. He is holding a handmade sign with 'HELP' written on it. He climbs onto the stage.

Can I . . .

*With a sign from the **Mother Superior**, the **Sisters** pounce. They take him down, beat him up and leave him quivering on the floor.*

Lost Brother   Sisters, please!

Sisters   We are not your sisters.

Lost Brother   I know that.

Mother Superior *gestures and the **Sisters** go in for more.*

Lost Brother   Please!

He is pinned to the ground.

Sisters   What do you want? Why are you here?

Lost Brother   I am looking for help.

Sisters   Help?

He manages to free a hand and hold up his sign.

Lost Brother   Yes. Help.

Sisters   Are you alone?

Lost Brother   Yes. I'm alone.

Mother Superior   At ease.

With a sign from the **Mother Superior***, the* **Sisters** *release him from their grip and back off.*

Lost Brother   Please can I stay? I have travelled for days (or is it years?) to find you. I am tired and hungry and need a bed for the night.

Mother Superior *looks down at her prey. She is like a Mafia boss.*

Lost Brother   Please . . .

He struggles with what to call this predatory icon.

I don't know what to call you.

Sisters   Mother Superior.

Lost Brother   Please . . . Mother Superior.

Mother Superior   We don't have guests at the Convent of the Three Fs.

Lost Brother   The Three Fs?

Sisters   Fearful, Fucked and Furious.

Mother Superior   You may stay, but not for long and not for free.

Lost Brother   I understand. I have money.

Mother Superior   I don't want your dirty money, son. I want your respect. So listen up and listen hard.

She strokes her beard.

Do you see this, son. Do you see my blue beard?

Lost Brother   Yes. I see it. I didn't want to mention it.

Mother Superior   Why not?

Lost Brother   I didn't want to be rude.

Mother Superior   Fuck off.

*The **Sisters** start to hum softly.*

Mother Superior   I wear this beard as a memory.
I wear it as a promise.
And I wear it as a warning.

Lost Brother   A warning? Of what? Tell me.

Mother Superior   You don't get to make demands.

Lost Brother   I wasn't . . .

Mother Superior   You don't get to call the shots.

Lost Brother   Please!

Mother Superior   Outside these walls is a world where
nothing and no one can be trusted. And I do not and will
not trust you. Understood?

Lost Brother   Understood.

Pause.

I don't know what to do . . . And I can't remember what to
call you . . .

Mother Superior   Mother Superior.

Lost Brother   Mother Superior.

Mother Superior   I'll tell you what you will do. You will
watch and you will listen and perhaps you will learn.

*The **Sisters** sing.*

Sisters
   We are the fearful, fucked and furious
   We looked evil in the eye
   Paid the price for being curious
   Were killed, but rise, and will not die.
   We made it home when others didn't.
   We slipped the noose and stayed alive

We got in, although forbidden
Made a bargain to survive.

Mother Superior *gets a shovel and starts to dig. The shovel hits* *something hard.*

Sisters
We are the fearful, fucked and furious
We looked evil in the eye
Paid the price for being curious
Were killed, but rise, and will not die.

Act One

Mother Superior *plants her hands in the dirt and uses all her strength to release the book from the grip of the earth. She pulls it out of its grave, brushes the soil off the cover and opens it. It is the story of Blue Beard. She starts to read.*

THE GOOD MAN

Mother Superior   Once there was a man who was kind to his core. 'I am born to serve,' he would laugh as, after a long day's work, he would cook for his wife and two daughters. He would joke and sing as he fed them treats and listened to their stories. They, coated in years of unconditional love, would roll their eyes, shake their heads and gently despair of their softhearted saviour. He asked nothing of them except that they be happy and free. And they did just that.

'Could such a man exist?' I hear you ask. Yes. Such a man did exist. My friend's friend's sister's friend's Capoeira teacher saw it with her own eyes.

But life is cruel. Or is it just life? No matter. One quiet, sunny afternoon the endangered species of good men suffered a body blow and the rare man died.

Three women appear. They stand by a coffin with a floral tribute spelling 'DAD' perched on top. They are a mother and two daughters. All wear black and hold a single red rose.

His passing was neither too sudden nor too slow. As if, even with his final rasping breath, he looked after them still, giving them enough time to say goodbye but not so much that their hearts would break forever.

Through her tears the **Mother** *thought to herself –*

Treasure   Who will now say I am beautiful in the mornings?

Mother Superior   The Good Man saw only her beauty, even when she had had sleep in her eyes, stretch marks on her belly and silver spittle on her downy chin.

Treasure *places a rose on his coffin.*

Mother Superior   In the harsh light of reality, the sister pondered –

Trouble   Who will now dust me with annoying and unconditional praise?

Mother Superior   The Good Man saw only his brilliant baby, even when she was teenage, stroppy and desperate to break free.

Trouble *places a rose on his coffin.*

Mother Superior   The other said only three short words.

Lucky   Thank you, Dad.

Mother Superior   The Good Man lavished so much love on this lucky creature that she became just that. Lucky. Not even death could take this priceless gift away from her.

Lucky *places a rose on his coffin.*

Mother Superior   Then, like glitter in a shaken snow globe, the women were forced to land without him.

The women re-form, taking new roles. Finally, **Treasure** *shakes herself free of their needy hugs.*

Treasure   Enough. He's gone. Time to look ahead.

Trouble *and* **Lucky** *look lost.*

Treasure   You know that is what he would have wanted. For us to move on.
Go away.
Just for a few hours.
Shoo.

Trouble *and* **Lucky**   Where to?

Treasure   To wherever your hearts desire.

Mother Superior   A book or a band,
A shop or a shed
An island or a slum –
They started to plan
Their new promised land
A world away from Mum.

Trouble *and* **Lucky** *teeter on the edge of a new chapter.*

Treasure   Stay safe.

Lucky *and* **Trouble**   We will.

Treasure   Now, go!

Trouble *and* **Lucky** *leave and* **Treasure** *crumbles.*

Mother Superior   The Mother. Once a wife and a lover,
looks at her big empty life.

From the moment they met, the Good Man had called her
'Treasure'. Treasure because he felt he had found her
glistening in a life otherwise filled with rubble. He felt
blessed to have found such bounty and knew in his heart
that he could never truly possess such a magnificent haul of
human wonder. As she read her book at night, he would
sneak a peek at her resting face and, through his half-shut
eye, marvel at this Aladdin's cave of surprise.

The **Mother** *pulls her husband's suit out of the wardrobe. She holds
it against her and tangles herself up in it.*

Mother Superior   Old habits die hard.

Treasure   He called me Treasure – but not anymore. I am
returned to the rubble.

THE LOST MAN

Mother Superior   Your turn. Tell us your story.

Lost Brother   You want me to . . .

Mother Superior   Yes. I want you to tell me your story.

Lost Brother   Once upon a time (or was it yesterday?), there was a big sister.

Mother Superior   That's enough.

Lost Brother   I thought you wanted me to –

Mother Superior   I changed my mind. Have you got a problem with that?

Lost Brother   No.

Mother Superior   Good.

THREE LITTLE RINGS

Lucky *and* **Trouble** *walk the streets. Still sad, but giddy with their newfound free fall.*

Mother Superior   Two sisters. Lucky and Trouble. They weren't christened that way but when the Good Man leant over their cots to say good night, love and delight beaming from his smiling eyes, these were the words that popped out.

'Lucky' and 'Trouble.'

The nicknames stuck and no one can now remember what they should have been called. Janice? Heather? Enid?

Best stick with the names that made the world (and their dad) smile. Lucky and Trouble. And they were just that.

They dance a little. Drink a little (although it is mostly **Trouble** *who likes a tipple). Laugh a little. Take their shoes off and skip a little.*

Mother Superior   Each was loved as dearly as the other and they were as tight as two musketeers.

Then they see a sign:

'Magic Tonight. Blue Beard.'

Trouble   Shall we?

Lucky   Mum will wonder where we are.

Mother Superior   Although, in truth, it was the Good Man who worried about his daughters, and he wasn't there anymore.

Lucky   Let's send the signal.

They go to the telephone box. Squeezing in as they dial.

We see **Treasure** *and* **Mother Superior** *stand by the phone, counting the rings.*

Mother Superior *and* **Treasure**   One
Two
Three . . .

The phone stops ringing and **Treasure** *and* **Mother Superior** *exhale with relief.*

Mother Superior   Three little rings. The only thing the Good Man had asked of them.

Lucky   He used to hold our hands to help us cross the road.

They laugh together.

Trouble *and* **Lucky**   When we were sixteen!

Trouble   I'd take his hand again now if I could.

Mother Superior   The warm shadow of the Good Man tickled them in winter drizzle and, in the absence of his hand to take, they took each other's.

Trouble *and* **Lucky** *sing and dance.*

THREE LITTLE RINGS

'Stay safe' he said.
'Stay home and warm.'
We laughed and said, 'Not yet.
We're fearless and strong,
And life is long,
And we'll quiver when we're dead'.

'But what if the bogey man gets you?' he said,
We smiled and said, 'Just try.
We're fierce and true,
We're black and we're blue,
We'll surrender when we die.'

Three little rings to say you love me,
Three little rings to say you care,
Three little rings to save my worries,
Indulge a father's prayer.

'Then let me know
You're safe' he said.
We winked and said 'OK,
We understand,
Your sweet command and we'll call at break of day.'

'No need to speak or stress' he said, 'I want you to be free,
Just send me a sign
A note or a line
And I'll sleep peacefully.'

Three little rings to say you love me,
Three little rings to say you care,
Three little rings to save my worries,
Indulge a father's prayer.

THE MAGICIAN

Blue Beard *enters through velvet curtains to a fanfare of cracked horns. The coffin follows magically in his wake. The tribute to 'DAD' has gone but the three roses are still atop.*

Blue Beard *bows.*

Blue Beard   Good evening, friends and good evening, enemies. (I can't believe that you are all friends and I don't want to miss anyone out.)

Lucky *and* **Trouble** *join the audience to watch.*

Blue Beard   Welcome to an evening of thrills and flutters.
Impossibilities and teases. Danger and death.
Did I say death? I meant meth.

He blows white powder out of his hand and breathes it in with a wild twinkle.

Mother Superior   Blue Beard.
Charming and elusive,
A creature without care.
A flutter of thrill,
He can instil
If he burrows into your hair.

Blue Beard *picks up the roses and hands them to* **Mother Superior**. *She winces as the thorns prick her hand.*

Blue Beard   You can try to work out what I do.
Or, you can just give in.
Go on.
Give in.

He claps and a glamorous showgirl appears from behind the coffin.

Please give a warm round of applause for my brave assistant.

The audience oblige, but the **Assistant** *doesn't smile.* **Blue Beard** *claps his hands and the* **Assistant** *falls to the ground as if she is dead. He brings her back to her feet and turns his gaze to the audience.*

Now. I need a volunteer.

Blue Beard *surveys the crowd and picks out* **Lucky**. *He beckons her onto the stage.* **Mother Superior** *tries to intervene, but* **Lucky** *is up for anything.*

Blue Beard   And what's your name, dear?

Lucky   Lucky.

Blue Beard   A big hand for our Plucky Lucky!

The audience applauds and **Lucky** *basks in the attention.*

Blue Beard   Let the magic begin!

Blue Beard *sings*.

Talent and Skill

I was born with a talent
I've turned into skill.
A pedestrian pulse that quickens at will.
I can spot 'em a mile off, the fickle, the weak,
I raise my sad eyes and give them a wink.

He puts **Lucky** *into a 'cut the lady in half' box.*

Sisters (*sing*)
His talent's to spot where the cracks reside
His skill is to give them good game
His craft is to strip them of instinct and pride
His task is to take great aim.

He cuts **Lucky** *in half.*

Blue Beard (*sings*)
I truly can't help it, can't change who I am
Am I not worth as much as the next bleating lamb?
I shan't say I'm sorry,
Will never say stop,
My gift is a spinning unbreakable top.

Sisters (*sing*)
His talent's to spot where the weaknesses lie
His skill is to bother and poke
His craft is to make them forget how they cry
His task is to make it a joke.

Lucky *emerges from the coffin in one piece. She is delighted!*

Blue Beard *claps his hands and* **Lucky** *falls backwards. He catches her like Clark Gable and looks deep into her eyes. He places her back on her feet.*

Blue Beard   One last round for my fabulous Lucky!

The audience clap and **Blue Beard** *sends her back to her seat.*

Blue Beard (*sings*)
>My talent, my skill, my craft, my task
>What a wonderful deck I possess,
>Until they are laid in a cold crushing cask
>I couldn't care for them less.

Sisters (*sing*)
>His talent's to pick out his prey from a crowd
>His skill is to pull her in strong.
>His craft is to make her forget who she is
>And never admit that he's wrong.

Blue Beard *places his* **Assistant** *against a target and throws knives at her. The last knife hits her in the forehead and blood trickles down her face. Did that just happen?*

The curtains close and **Blue Beard** *bows, leading the audience in laughter and applause. He throws a red rose to* **Lucky** *who catches it with delight.*

He turns the 'Magic Tonight' sign around to reveal a new message. 'Wanted. Magician's Assistant'. **Blue Beard** *winks.*

THE TRAP

Lucky *and* **Trouble** *approach* **Blue Beard** *as he is clearing up his instruments of torture. He gives* **Trouble** *the creeps and her instincts jangle but still he weaves his spell.*

Trouble   We should go.

Lucky   Not yet.

Blue Beard   Are you interested?

Trouble   No we're not.

Lucky   If I was interested . . .

Trouble   Which she's not.

Lucky   IF I was . . .

Blue Beard   Interested . . .

Lucky   Yes . . .

Trouble   No . . .

Blue Beard   If . . .

Lucky   If . . .

Blue Beard   You would meet me here tomorrow. At noon.

Trouble   For fuck's sake. No one is meeting anyone tomorrow. Come on!

Trouble *tries to get away, but* **Blue Beard** *grabs her arm. There is a collective sharp intake of breath.*

Blue Beard   I'm sorry. I just didn't want you to fall.

He releases his grip and she falls into his arms. He catches her. It's Clark Gable again.

He puts **Trouble** *back on her feet and the spell is (almost) broken.*

Blue Beard   It's up to you. I'll be here. Tomorrow. Noon.

Lucky *and* **Trouble** *slowly back away.*

Blue Beard   Why don't you both come? In fact, bring your mother. The more the merrier. I'll surprise you all with a day out. It's up to you, but remember, life is for living.

Mother Superior   Even bad men say good things.

Blue Beard *disappears and* **Treasure** *appears.*

Treasure   He's right my vivid ones. Life IS for living.

THE BIG SISTER

Mother Superior   Boy!

Lost Brother   Yes . . . What do I call you?

Mother Superior   Mother Superior.

Lost Brother   Mother Superior. It's hard to get used to.

Mother Superior   I need a break. Your turn. Tell me your story.

Lost Brother   Are you sure?

Mother Superior *gestures for him to continue.*

Mother Superior   You were telling us about the Big Sister.

Lost Brother   Yes. I was. The Big Sister. She was single-minded and brave and took it upon herself to bash down the undergrowth of family expectations to clear the way for her little brother to skip freely wherever he wanted.

The **Lost Sister** *appears. She has black hair and dark heavily made-up eyes. She wears no colour.*

Lost Sister   I didn't do it for you.

Lost Brother   She said.

Lost Sister   I did it because it had to be done.

Lost Brother   She longed only to be free. But freedom is a slippery fucker when you are young.

Lost Sister   And a girl.

Lost Brother   Shut up. This is my story.

Lost Sister   That's what you think!

Lost Brother   And she tapped him on the wrong side of the shoulder to make him turn for nothing. By day the Big Sister worked, but by night she painted her face and sang as if her heart would burst.

(*To* **Lost Sister**.) Why do you wear so much make up?

Lost Sister   To cover my pain.

Lost Brother   She replied. And she crossed her eyes, stuck out her tongue and gave him a wedgy.

Lost Sister   For old time's sake.

Lost Brother   I hate you.

Lost Sister   Not as much as I hate you.

Lost Brother   She laughed as she went back to the mirror. The Little Brother hovered behind her, checking out his own reflection next to hers.

Mother Superior   Did he like what he saw?

Lost Brother   What?

Mother Superior   The Little Brother. In the mirror. Did he like his reflection?

Lost Brother   I don't know.

Mother Superior   I bet he did. And that, boy, is the trouble with men. You can never get to the bathroom mirror.

THE DAY OUT

In a fabulous fog of smoke and mirrors, **Blue Beard** *appears*.

Blue Beard   Ladies! You came!

Mother Superior   Why would they not?

Treasure, **Trouble** *and* **Lucky**   Life is for living.

Blue Beard *magics three red headscarves. One for each of them.*

Blue Beard   Put these on.

Lucky   I like my hair how it is, thank you.

Blue Beard   So do I, but I don't want to ruin it. Chop chop!

Blue Beard *claps and the women put on their scarves.*

Mother Superior   Little Red Riding Hoods all.

Treasure   How did you know we would come?

Blue Beard   Why would you not? Life is for living.

Trouble   And there is safety in numbers.

Blue Beard *smiles at* **Trouble**.

Blue Beard   Wise girl.

To all.

But there is nothing to be scared of – except unbearable and exquisite pleasure!

Mother Superior   And with a whip and a wallop he whisked them out of their ordinary lives. Once heavy with grief and routine he presented our wobbly trio with three horses wild.

Treasure *looks up at the beasts and laughs.*

Treasure   What about helmets and saddles?

Blue Beard   What about them?

Blue Beard *magics a small screen. Horses appear animated on it, wild and running free. The women watch in delight as* **Mother Superior** *narrates.*

Mother Superior   And like a makeshift ring master, Blue Beard led them out of their small town. They looked down from their hairy equine perches at streets familiar. He paraded them through suburbs, modest Godivas all – and they loved it. They waved like royalty at puzzled neighbours and giggled like toddlers as their horses flicked and farted. The ever-narrowing lanes and alleyways squeezed, snagged and suffocated them until – pop! They were birthed into open space.

The women get up and breathe deep and slow.

Delicious, intoxicating and longed for space.

They shout with abandon.

How they whooped with joy and relief!

They dance and run.

The women guzzled the cool air and swung their lazy ribcages with a newfound thirst for freedom.

Blue Beard *opens a flask and pours liquid into three mugs.*

Mother Superior *tries to take the flask from him, but he dodges her grasp.*

Treasure, Trouble *and* **Lucky** *drink like thirsty children,* **Trouble** *holds her mug up for more.* **Blue Beard** *obliges.*

Mother Superior   Whatever was in that flask tasted as sweet as the cold tap at 4am after a salty kebab. Bad cats.

Blue Beard   So? Are you enjoying your day out? Was it worth the risk?

The women smile.

Mother Superior   Look at the smug pride of the gamblers.

Treasure   I thought I would never laugh again.

Trouble   Is there more to drink?

Lucky   I love it. All of it.

All three begin to sway.

Blue Beard *produces coloured ribbons and teases the women with them – like kittens they pounce and chase. He gives them a ribbon each and they make circles of joy in the air.* **Treasure** *starts to feel strange.*

Treasure   We should think about going home.

Lucky *and* **Trouble**   No!

Blue Beard   Your mother is right. Now, where is that horse?

Blue Beard *claps his hands and the women become a horse that he rides home. Picnic mugs become hooves and a ribbon is gripped in* **Treasure**'s *mouth like a bridle. It is disturbing, sexual and over in a minute.*

Did we just see that?

THE SEDUCTION

Treasure, **Lucky** *and* **Trouble** *collapse in a messy heap on the floor.*

Mother Superior   The woozy women slept, tamed by torpor. In the fuzzy half-light, Blue Beard surveyed his bounty and slipped into the private space between slumber and stocking tops.

He explores their nonconsenting bodies. He touches a face. He slips off a shoe and rubs a foot.

Silly Sleeping beauties all!

He peeps under a skirt. **Mother Superior** *blows her whistle.*

Wake up!

Blue Beard *goes for her.*

Blue Beard   Be quiet old lady.

Blue Beard *snatches the book from* **Mother Superior**. **Mother Superior** *snatches the book back and there is an undignified scuffle.* **Blue Beard** *wins but hands the book back to* **Mother Superior** *with a bow. He is not scared of her. He puts his finger to his lips as a warning.*

His gaze returns to the sleeping women.

Blue Beard   How unique these creatures think they are, and yet how frustratingly predictable.

He rifles through **Treasure**'s *handbag and empties the contents all over them. Hooligan!*

Blue Beard   Cut them open and all I see are shabby pants, perfume and dirty lipstick stubs.

THE TRICK

They wake, back in their house. Nothing is where it should be.

Mother Superior   The morning after.
Heads hurt,
Stomachs turn,
And instincts jangle.

The women try to piece themselves and their clothes together.

Mother Superior   Skin creeps and shoulders roll
Like the memory of an unwanted touch.

Mother Superior *blows her whistle.*

WAKE UP!

Trouble   Oh God

Mother Superior   I hate the morning after.

Trouble   I need a drink

Mother Superior   Me too.

Treasure   Drink is the last thing we need.

Lucky   Does anyone remember how we got home?

Trouble   Taxi?

Treasure   Perhaps we walked?

Lucky   It doesn't feel like we walked.

They all try to remember the night before.

Mother Superior   Things that seemed funny now seem
peculiar. Things that were said – sound odd.

Treasure   I don't want you seeing him again.
Where's my necklace?

Trouble   It's here. I am wearing it . . .

Treasure   Why?

Trouble   I don't know. Here . . .

Lucky   I want to see him again. You can't stop me.

Treasure   No one is stopping anybody doing anything.

Trouble   It sounded like you were.

Treasure   It was a turn of phrase. I don't want to be rude, I just don't like him . . .

Lucky   Well perhaps he doesn't like you, Mother. Where's my shoe?

Mother Superior   Sloppy Cinderella.

Treasure   Here.

Lucky   I like him. I had fun.

Trouble   This isn't what fun feels like.

Trouble *lights a cigarette and shares it with* **Treasure**.

There is a knock at the door.

It is **Blue Beard** *with a bunch of red roses.*

Lucky   Come in.

Treasure *and* **Trouble**   No!

Lucky   Yes!

Lucky *and* **Blue Beard** *lock eyes.*

THE SELECTION

Mother Superior   Desire is a tricky fucker.

There is nothing anyone can do about it. You can judge all you like but, once it has taken hold, there is no pulling the powerful tick off.

Blue Beard *goes down on one knee.* **Lucky** *takes the flowers. They choose each other.*

Treasure *and* **Trouble** *stand behind like fucked-up bridesmaids.*

Lucky   Be happy for me. I know what I want, and I know what I am doing.

The band strikes up and the **Dead Assistant** *appears.*

WHEN YOU'RE LUCKY

Dead Assistant (*sings*)
> When you're lucky there's nothing to scare you.
> When you're loved there is nothing to fear
> When the Gods rain down glitter and honey
> The path of life is clear.

> When you're blessed the world is sunlit
> Hope shines clear, bright and true
> When ahead lie only adventures
> Skies all shimmering blue

> But what will you do when the luck runs out, dear?
> What will you do when it fails?
> Where are your dreams when the magic explodes?
> Will you dig through the dirt with your nails?

THE MARRIAGE

Blue Beard *and* **Lucky** *walk down the aisle. The wedding is more Fellini than Richard Curtis.*

Blue Beard *and* **Lucky**   I, take thee, to be my wedded wonder, to have and to hold, for richer, for poorer, in sickness and in health, to love and to cherish, till death do us part.

Lucky *throws her bouquet and* **Mother Superior** *catches it. The happy couple dance with ease and joy.*

The **Dead Assistant** *sings:*

> Every stranger could be a lover
> Each shock a leap of joy.

Nothing can hurt the sweet lucky blossom
That opens like a toy.
Better wise up, young one
Better get down and get low
No one is lucky forever
Beware the undertow.

But what will you do when the luck runs out, dear?
What will you do when it fails?
Where are your dreams when the magic explodes?
Will you dig through the dirt with your nails?

Mother Superior   If you asked them later who was at the wedding, who was cheering them on and who was crying in the vestry – they wouldn't be able to answer. Love. The perfect set of fluffy black blinkers.

Dead Assistant (*sings*)
    With your nails!

The world vanishes and leaves the newlyweds in the privacy of the marital bedroom.

THE WEDDING NIGHT

Blue Beard   Hello.

Lucky   Hello.

Blue Beard   Welcome to your new home.

Lucky   Oh! It's massive.
It's beautiful!

Blue Beard   Would you like the grand tour? There's lots more to see.

Lucky   The tour can wait. I'm happy to stay here.

Blue Beard   The bedroom?

Lucky   The bedroom

Blue Beard *smiles. He is in no rush.*

Lucky   Tell me everything. I want to know everything. Feel everything.

Blue Beard   My gorgeous greedy girl

Lucky   Tell me your story.

Blue Beard   You don't need to know my story.

Lucky   But I do.

DEEP DARK BLUE HAIR

Blue Beard (*sings*)
  My mother said that,
  When I was born
  A shock of blue hair appeared on my crown.
  Deep Dark Blue hair
  Perched upon my crown,
  Flowed like water,
  Soft as eiderdown,
  Deep dark blue on my crown.

Sisters (*sing*)
  Oh! He must be touched by the devil, they cried.
  Oh! I must be a blue-blooded prince, he replied.

Blue Beard (*speaking*)   I was born with a shock of blue hair. Aghast, the nurses froze in horror. 'It's not mine' my father cried, as he swung a drunken punch. 'You must have dropped your knickers for a blue-headed monster, you dirty slapper.' But mother ducked and shrugged, she'd developed quick reflexes over the years. 'You don't believe me whatever I say, so I'm saying nothing.' Father threw the wet umbrella that was hung on the inside of the delivery room door directly at my head. But mother, quick as a flash, caught it.

Mother Superior *throws an umbrella.* **Blue Beard** *catches it and opens it over his head.*

Blue Beard   'I will protect you, my special blue boy.'

Lucky   Mothers love you no matter what you are.

Blue Beard   And she did. She loved me and fed me until the blue down fell out. Indigo fur on my lily-white pillow.

Blue Beard *holds the umbrella over* **Lucky**. *They take it in turns to protect each other.*

Lucky   And what did your father say?

Blue Beard (*sings*)
My father said that
When my voice did drop
Blue sprouts appeared on my pale and boyish breast.
Deep Dark Blue,
Coarse upon my chest.
Thick as treacle,
Sharp as lemon zest,
Deep dark blue on my chest.

Sisters (*sing*)
Oh! He must be touched by a beast, they cried.
Oh! I must be a blue-blooded king, he replied.

Blue Beard (*speaking*)   My father couldn't look at me.

Mother Superior *throws a bottle.* **Blue Beard** *catches it.*

Blue Beard   'All I see is dirty blue.'

Blue Beard *raises the bottle as if to strike, but* **Lucky** *grabs the bottle and places a calming hand on his chest.*

Lucky   Fathers fight their sons no matter what.

Blue Beard   And he did. He pushed, poked and punched the blue out of me. Indigo stains on my milky-white sheets.

Lucky *runs her fingers over his hairy chest.*

Lucky   So, when did it grow back, my hirsute husband?

Blue Beard   You do know there were others before you?

Lucky   I know.

Blue Beard   And if I talk of them, you won't feel threatened?

Lucky   I am not made of glass. I know I am loved and wanted. And I know I am lucky.

Blue Beard   You are.

They drink the wine.

Lucky *straddles* **Blue Beard** *and tries to shake intimacy out of him.*

Lucky   You still haven't answered me! When did it grow?

Blue Beard   What?

Lucky   Your beautiful bright blue beard? Tell me everything.

Blue Beard   I like to have my secrets.

Lucky   Secrets are good. But not tonight.

Blue Beard *grabs her and throws her onto her back. She laughs.*

Blue Beard   I don't want to hurt you.

Lucky *wraps her legs around him.*

Lucky   You won't. Tell me.

Blue Beard   Even if it stings?

Lucky   Especially if it stings.

They make love. It is deep, true and intimate without artifice.
Mother Superior *protects their modesty by covering them with an umbrella.*

Blue Beard (*sings*)
　　My first wife said that
　　When I was spent
　　My hair turned blue as I closed my cold grey eyes.
　　Deep Dark Blue
　　Chin, arms and thighs

    Spread like ivy
    Blue as butterflies
    Deep dark blue on my thighs.

Sisters (*sing*)
    Oh! You must be touched by my love, she cried.
    Oh! I must be a blue-blooded God, he replied.

Blue Beard *rolls away and lights a cigarette. He holds it for*
Lucky. *She smokes as he talks.*

Blue Beard   On my first wedding night, empty and full in
equal measure, my beard turned blue before my first wife's
eyes.

She stroked it, licked it and tugged at it, but it wouldn't
budge. It wouldn't fall out.

Lucky   Wives like to meddle.

Lucky *reaches over to touch his beard, but he catches her hand
before it lands.*

Blue Beard   In the nourishing soil of the marital bed, my
blue hair took root. And it cannot now be changed.

Lucky   I don't want to change it.

Blue Beard   My first wife said that I must have been
touched by her love.

Lucky   And now you are touched by mine.

Blue Beard   Talking time is over. Sleep.

Lucky   Good night, husband.

Blue Beard   Shhhhh

Lucky *falls asleep, open like a trusting cat.*

Mother Superior   And what do you say, Blue Beard?

Blue Beard   I say that blue now runs through my veins
forever. Deep dark blue rage bubbling until it overflows.

Mother Superior   And what do you think, Blue Beard?

Blue Beard   I think I must be a fucking God.

Sisters (*sing*)
Deep Dark Blue Hair
Coarse thick blue hair
Deep Dark Blue
Upon his crown.

LEAVE ME ALONE

The **Lost Brother** *sits on a bean bag. He is playing a video game.*
Mother Superior *watches.*

Lost Brother   Once upon a time (or was it last year?) the
Little Brother played video games until his thumbs bled.
Digits whirring, he stepped into the skin of a medieval
assassin, diving from tall buildings before punching passing
wenches that delayed his escape. He was free. He was
invincible. He whooped with exhilaration as chickens and
stray dogs were kicked out of his path.

Mother Superior   Caves, sheds and rooms
Walls, roofs and tombs
Men and boys
Shut out the noise,
Else they'd be consumed.

WHERE THE WILD THINGS ARE

Lost Brother (*sings*)
Where the wild things are
Is scary and dark.
Take me away
Take me away
Where the mad things are
Is strange and stark.
Leave me alone

Oh, leave me alone
Oh, leave me in a world
Where my falls cannot hurt.
Where I take a hit without crying
Hide me in a place where the bad disappear
High in the sky, I am flying.

Mother Superior *looks down at the dreaming, anxious boy.*

Mother Superior   Wakey, wakey, fella. Snap out of whatever dream you're wallowing in.

She picks up his socks and shoes and throws them at him.

Tidy yourself up. We are a proud people here at the Convent of the Three Fs.

Sisters   Fearful, Fucked and Furious!

Lost Brother   I will. Sorry. I was just . . .

Mother Superior   Just what? Wasting your life in a self-pitying stupor? Nothing?

Lost Brother   You're terrifying.

Mother Superior   Good. Now carry on.

Lost Brother   With?

Mother Superior   Not the video game or that bloody song . . . Your story! Continue.

Lost Brother   One night last summer (or was it a lifetime ago?), the Big Sister had a gig.

(*To the* **Lost Sister**.) Does it count as a gig if only three people, a whippet and digestive biscuit come?

Lost Sister   Yes. If you get to eat the biscuit.

Lost Brother   She always wore black. Nothing else would do. Only a punch of red interrupted her sartorial grief, smeared thick on her humming lips.

(*To* **Lost Sister**.) Why do you always wear black?

Lost Sister   It's my coat of armour. It keeps the bad people away.

Lost Brother   It doesn't keep me away.

Lost Sister   More's the bloody pity.

Lost Brother   And she pinned him to the floor and tapped him on the forehead until he begged for mercy.

(*To* **Lost Sister**.) Get off me!

Lost Sister   Then get out of my room!

Lost Brother   She laughed as she started to dance.

On the other side of the door, the **Little Brother** *watched her through the crack.*

Lost Sister   I know you're out there, Stinkbomb.

Lost Brother (*to the* **Lost Sister**)   I'm not!

And they laughed in sibling harmony. The big sister never fully closed the door, the key was never turned. She let the little brother roam freely although he never thanked her for it.

Lost Sister   I didn't cut down the forest for nothing.

Lost Brother (*sings*)
  Where the sad things are
  Is outside this door.
  Hide me away,
  Hide me away,
  Where the chaos waits
  Is one breath more.
  Leave me here,
  Oh, leave me here,
  Leave me in a world where my falls
  Cannot hurt,
  Where I take a hit without crying.
  Hide me in a place where the bad disappear.
  High in the sky,
  I am flying.

The **Lost Sister** *packs up what she needs for her gig.*

THE TEST

Blue Beard *is getting dressed. He combs his beard and does up his trousers.* **Lucky** *appears wearing only a man's shirt. She throws her arms around him.*

Blue Beard   My darling girl. I have to go away.

Lucky   No! Stay here with me.

Blue Beard   You know I want to.

They are like hungry eels as they wriggle into each other's secret places.

Lucky   Then come back to bed.

Mother Superior   No one wants the first bubble of buttery bliss to burst.

Blue Beard (*to* **Mother Superior**)   But burst it must.

(*To* **Lucky**.) Someone has to keep us in cocktails, candles and caviar.

Mother Superior   I've always been happy with a Babycham and a Twiglet.

Blue Beard   I'll be away for a while. So have fun, special one.

Lucky   I won't have any fun without you.

Blue Beard   I doubt that.

Mother Superior   Blue Beard explains the rules.

Blue Beard   In that there are none!

He clicks his fingers and there is an explosion of joy – or is it just a confetti cannon? **Lucky** *delights in his carefree love.*

THE WALK TO WORK

The **Lost Sister** *walks to her gig. She wears a distinctive coat and carries a guitar case.*

THE BARGAIN

Blue Beard *produces a bunch of keys from thin air and seductively works his way through each key.*

Mother Superior   Blue Beard tells Lucky that the house is hers and that she should explore it freely.
The kitchen, the wardrobe, the safe and the vault
The lounge, the bath and the bed
The library, the club, the laundry, the snug
And the morgue for when you are dead.

Blue Beard *goes to leave but just before he closes the door, he remembers something.*

Blue Beard   Oh!

He pauses.

There is one room that you must not go in to.

Mother Superior *tries to blow her whistle, but no sound comes out of it.*

Blue Beard *holds out his hand to ask for the keys back.* **Lucky** *feels the temperature change.*

Mother Superior *tries to blow her whistle again, but still no sound comes out of it.*

Lucky *places the keys back in his hand and he singles out one golden key. He takes it off the ring and holds it up.*

Blue Beard   This one must never be used. Do you understand?

Lucky   I understand.

Blue Beard   Understanding is one thing, but do you agree?

Mother Superior   What bargains we accept when cornered by desire.

Lucky   I agree.

Blue Beard   Good girl.

He kisses her on her forehead and places the bunch of keys back in her hand. With a blow, he lets go of the small key and it hangs magically in the air. He slowly wags his finger and leaves.

Lucky *is left by herself. She is happy and plays with the keys with only a sneaky look at the forbidden one, hanging in the air.*

Lucky (*sings*)
    When you're lucky there's nothing to scare you.
    When you're loved there is nothing to fear
    When the Gods rain down glitter and honey
    The path of life is clear.

    When you're blessed the world is sunlit
    Hope shines clear, bright and true
    When ahead lie only adventures
    Skies all shimmering blue.

Mother Superior   There is nothing sadder than an unshared pleasure.

The **Lost Sister** *makes a call from her mobile.*

Lucky *goes to the phone and dials.*

Lost Sister   I'm here, Mum.

Lucky   Hello, Trouble.

Lost Sister   Yes, Mum. I'm safe.

Lucky   He's gone away on business . . . and it's bloody wonderful here!

Lost Sister   No. I won't be late home.

Lucky   Come over. And bring Mum. She needs cheering up and we've got the house to ourselves!

Lost Sister (*laughing*)   OK! I'll try my best!

Lucky   Come on!

Lucky *and* **Lost Sister**   It'll be brilliant!

Lucky   Is your nose a-twitching, blossom?
Are your ears a-tuned to the threat?
Is your heart big enough to withstand the break
Your chalk hands free of sweat?

THE SLEEPOVER

There is a knock at the door and **Lucky** *opens it.* **Trouble** *is
holding two bottles of spirits and wears a party hat.* **Treasure** *also
wears a party hat, but with less conviction.*

Lucky *jangles the keys and the women scream with delight and
anticipation. What fun.*

Mother Superior   Let the games begin!

The **Lost Sister** *starts her gig.*

Lost Sister   Hello, Bath! . . . Hello, Bath! I wanna hear you
make some noise!
That's more like it.
This one is for all the girls in the room. And I mean all of
you.

Lucky, **Trouble** *and* **Treasure** *whoop*!

GIRLS GIRLS GIRLS

Lost Sister (*sings*)
    Oh! Yeah, yeah, yeah, yeah, yeah,
    Give me someone soft and loud
    Someone fast and proud
    Oh! Yeah, yeah, yeah, yeah, yeah
    You'll be never truly mine
    Shivers down my spine
    Oh yeah, I want to laugh and dance and cry,
    Oh yeah, I turn my face up to the sky.

    Oh! Girls, girls, girls, girls, girls
    We're so easily betrayed

Watch out for his blade
Oh! Girls, girls, girls, girls, girls
Hold on for your life
Resist the pain and strife
Oh yeah, I want to laugh and dance and cry,
Oh yeah I turn my face up to the sky.

In **Blue Beard**'*s castle, female freedom is expressed and enjoyed.
There is comfort and confidence and the women open and enjoy
every door and every pleasure.*

*They dress up and deny themselves nothing. They are excessive and
fearless. Oh, the joy of hedonism!* **Trouble** *dresses up in some kind
of bunny girl outfit. She takes the keys and opens a door. Behind it
are many beautiful bottles of booze!*

Mother Superior   The thing about women is . . .

Trouble   I can't resist a drink.

Mother Superior   The blur and the buzz,
The fizz and the fuzz
Watch their instincts sink.

Trouble *mixes herself a large cocktail. She is expert and knows what
she is doing.*

THEY CALL ME TROUBLE

Trouble (*sings*)
    They call me Trouble
    I dance on the rubble
    Born to puzzle, poke and break
    I smash what destroys me
    Trash what annoys me
    Bullshit I burn at the stake.

    Don't pour oil on my waters
    Or shelter your daughters
    Sand down my corners, explain
    My mess and my joy and my pain.

Trouble (*speaks*)   When I was young, my dad promised that, on my eighteenth birthday, he would take me to the pub and treat me to all the delicious drinks that were now at my disposal. He told me that wine made food and life taste sweeter and that beer would taste bitter at first. But he told me to be patient. Give it time, he said.

She drinks her cocktail.

He never took me to the pub. Not because he went back on his word or forgot, but because, by the time I was eighteen I had drunk every bar in town dry. He was right. Wine eases everything and bitterness grows on you.

(*Sings.*)
   Vivid not calm
   A cause for alarm
   They wish I was easy, sweet but no
   I like my rough edges
   My wild untrimmed hedges
   Pulled by my own undertow.

   Don't pour oil upon my waters
   Or shelter your daughters
   Sand down my corners, explain
   I'm hot, raging, thirsty, I'm greedy, I'm sad
   I'm so fucking angry I'm boiling hot mad
   I'm Troublesome bothersome popping my bubblegum –
   Stop!

   They call me Trouble!

Lost Sister   I'm in a bit of trouble at the moment. Nothing bad, nothing dramatic – but trouble nonetheless. Most mornings I wake up feeling a bit lost.

She thinks about that for a while then comes back to the room.

But tonight, you're making me feel found. And that is really good. Really good.

Treasure *takes the keys and opens a door. Behind it is a fridge laden with delicious delights.*

Mother Superior   The thing about women is . . .

Treasure *licks her lips and starts to tuck in.*

Treasure   I love a treat.

Mother Superior   The sugar the salt
Cashmere and malt
Watch their powers deplete.

Treasure   Always have. Licking the cake mixture off the spoon or the burn bits from the dish, having my feet rubbed or the touch of cold satin on my skin. When I got married it was a festival of treats – the rings, the party, the frock, the honeymoon, the attention and the man. The man who denied me nothing. The man who ran my baths, cheered me on and who, from the moment we met, never once looked at another woman.

She licks her plate clean.

The **Lost Sister** *sings another one.*

Lost Sister   Ever eaten too much? Drank too much?
Wanted too much?
Well, this one is for you.

GREEDY GIRLS

Lost Sister (*sings*)
   Greedy girls
   Voracious birds
   Insatiable lasses
   Tuck in!
   Fill your boots,
   And feed your roots
   From your teeth to your heart
   To your skin!

> Why not,
> my loves?
> Why not, I cry?
> Be wild, be true
> Be brave!
> Live long and live loud
> Stand out from the crowd
> For it's still and it's dark
> In your grave.

Through the song, **Lucky** *has taken the keys and opened a wardrobe full of gorgeous women's clothes. She rifles through the outfits without asking herself who they might have belonged to. She dresses as a Pierrot.*

Mother Superior   The thing about women is . . .

Lucky   I love clothes.

Mother Superior   The feel, the look
The path not took
Fantasy not prose.

Lucky   I love clothes. When I was little, I had those paper dollies that you could dress up in cardboard dresses with tabs. With a cut and a fold, a simple sketch would be transformed. From a shepherdess to a princess, a ballerina to a nurse. I graduated to my mother's clothes, shoes slopping as I walked the path of another. I would swirl and dance as I dreamt of lives un-lived and adventures yet to come. I could be anything. And I still can. You just have to press the tabs over your shoulders and dance the dance of another.

All the women, dance and drink and eat and sing. What messy, glorious, painful and personal joy!

Lost Sister (*sings*)
> Drink your fill,
> Live life to the full
> Why shouldn't you see

Every room?
Make your own choices
Howl with your voices
For it's quiet and cold
In your tomb.

Greedy girls
Voracious birds
Insatiable lasses
Tuck in!
Fill your boots,
And feed your roots
From your teeth to your heart
To your skin!
From your teeth to your heart
To your skin!
From your teeth to your heart
From your tits to your parts
From your teeth to your heart to your skin.

Treasure, **Lucky** and **Trouble** *find a red door. The last door. None of the keys fit. Drunk, fearless and full, they all look up at the floating key.*

Mother Superior *tries in vain to blow her whistle.*

Lucky *pulls down the forbidden key and holds it like a tiny Excalibur.*

Finally, **Mother Superior**'s *whistle works. She blows but it is too late.*

The lights snap to black.

Interval.

Act Two

We are back at the Convent of the Fearful, Fucked and Furious. The **Sisters** *sing.*

Sisters
We are the fearful, fucked and furious
We've looked evil in the eye
Paid the price for being curious
Were killed, but rise, and will not die.

We ran away and kept on running
We locked the doors and curled uptitght
We made the calls, used our cunning
Built these walls to keep out night.

We are the fearful, fucked and furious
We've looked evil in the eye
Paid the price for being curious
Were killed, but rise, and will not die.

Mother Superior   Welcome back to the Convent of the Three Fs

Sisters   Fearful, Fucked and Furious.

Mother Superior (*to the audience*)   I can't hear you, sisters!

Sisters   Fearful, Fucked and Furious!

Mother Superior   Bad bargains. We all make them. I'm not talking about buying a 'deep-filled baguette' only to discover it's a crusty tunnel of lies – we've all been there. I'm talking about the personal bargains, the sneaky deals we make that nag at our very edges.

We can hear the whistle blowing in the distance, but we brush aside our doubts and keep plodding along that well-known path. The path of least resistance.

But we are fools to think that these bargains have no consequence. That there will be no penalty for our lack of rigour. They chip away at our very souls and push us down. They crush our spirits, cauterize our joy and trap us on the slow and never-ending path towards devastating loss . . .

She looks round at the traumatised faces of the **Sisters**.

Too much?

Sisters   Maybe . . .

Mother Superior   Fair enough. Did you know that my mother had five legs?

Sisters   What?

Mother Superior   Her tights fitted her like a glove.

The **Sisters** *laugh and get back to their work.*

The **Lost Sister** *is packing up her stuff.*

Lost Brother   Can I help?

Lost Sister   Aren't you forgetting something?

Lost Brother   What?

Lost Sister   My gig. My songs. My bleeding heart on my ripped sleeve?

Lost Brother   Oh, that.

Lost Sister   Well? Did you enjoy it?

Lost Brother   It was good. If you like that sort of thing.

The **Lost Sister** *shakes her head.*

Lost Brother   And I do.

Lost Sister   What?

Lost Brother   Like that sort of thing.

Lost Sister   Thanks.

In an uncharacteristic display of affection, she gives him a hug. The **Lost Brother** *pushes her away and wriggles like he's been hugged by a snail.*

Lost Brother   Don't. People might see . . .

The **Lost Sister** *shrugs and picks up her things.*

Lost Brother   Walk you home?

Lost Sister   No. I want a drink and a look at the stars.

Lost Brother   I could join you?

Lost Sister   No. I want some peace and quiet.

Lost Brother   Fair.

Lost Sister   It meant a lot that you came. I know I'm a mess at the moment – but when I am up there singing it all starts to make a bit more sense. I like that you saw that.

That you see me.

Lost Brother   Oh God, I hate it when you get all deep on me.

Lost Sister   Go away then.

Lost Brother   I will. Fuck you.

Lost Sister   Fuck you!

The moment of affection has passed and habitual hostility crashes in. **Lost Brother** *walks home.*

The **Lost Sister** *opens a can of beer and looks at the stars. She breathes deep and exhales. There is a sorrow about her.*

Lost Sister   Fuck everyone.

(*She sings to the stars.*)

Why not,
my loves?
Why not, I cry?
Be wild, be true

Be brave!
Live long and live loud
Stand out from the crowd
For it's still and it's dark
In your grave.

THE PRICE

The curtains open to reveal **Lucky**, **Trouble** *and* **Treasure**. *They are outside the red door and present a tableau of horror.*

Mother Superior   Remember what I said about bargains? In that forbidden room, that locked chamber of horror, the three women realised the price of the bargains they had unwittingly made. The bodies of the wives that came before were stacked high in that nightmare cell. This was no fairy tale. Legs, arms, skulls, torsos, toes, blood, bone and gristle. Picture it.
Try harder.
Imagine the stench of decay, the sticky floor, clumps of matted hair, frantic scratches on the wall and the halting buzz of flies.
Enough.

For it is impossible to imagine what Lucky, Treasure and Trouble saw that terrible night.

The thing that sticks in my gullet is how those lifeless bodies were dispatched with no care. In death they were severed, scattered and stacked. As if they were not people at all. As if they didn't have hopes, dreams and struggles.

As if they were not loved.

She is lost in her own thoughts for a moment then snaps herself out of it.

Time to wake the fuck up.

Mother Superior *blows her whistle and the tableau comes to quivering life.*

The women are changed. Mascara runs down their faces as the tears fall. They are shocked, speechless, shaking and terrified. All we hear is their breath as they try to comprehend what they have just seen.

Lucky *feels something strange and looks down at the key in her hand. She lets out a gasp.*

Treasure   What is it?

Trouble   Don't say anything. I don't want to know.

THE BLEEDING KEY

Mother Superior   The key had started to bleed.

Lucky *shows the key to her* **Mother** *and* **Trouble** *who recoil in horror.*

Mother Superior   It was only a few drops at first, but the drops soon turned into a trickle.

Lucky *puts the bleeding key in her pocket.*

Mother Superior   The trickle turned into a squirt.

The blood seeps through her Pierrot's costume until she is red from head to toe.

And the squirt to a raging unstoppable torrent.

The women panic. They wrap the key in a towel, but the towel turns red. They get cloths and try to mop up the blood, but to no avail.

Mother Superior   They say the truth will out, and this little truth will not go quietly.

Treasure *opens the floor to reveal a pool of water.*

Mother Superior   If only one could put an inconvenient truth out of its misery.

The three women plunge the key into the water. It seems to thrash but they hold it down until it is still. They sit back, drenched and exhausted from the fight.

Lucky   Go home. You were never here.

Trouble   But, Lucky, the mess.

Treasure   Quickly.

The women get black bin bags and clear up the debris of horror and pleasure. Bottles, balloons and blood.

Lucky   Leave.

Trouble   Come with us. You're not safe here.

Lucky   I'll be fine. He loves me.

Treasure   He is not capable of love.

Lucky   He's my husband!

Treasure   If you need us. Call. Three rings. Not to say you are safe, but to say you are not.

Trouble *and* **Treasure** *put the bin liners outside the back door and* **Lucky** *pushes them away.*

Treasure *and* **Trouble** *melt into the night.*

THE WAY HOME

Lost Brother   When we were little, we were both rehearsed in what to say if we were lost. We learned our address.

The **Sisters** *recite their childhood addresses.*

Lost Brother   Our car number plate.

The **Sisters** *recite their childhood number plates.*

Lost Brother   And drilled to always say 'please'.

Sisters   Please.

Lost Brother   'Thank you'.

Sisters   Thank you.

Lost Brother   And to always ask a grown up for help if we needed it.

Sisters   Help.

Lost Brother   We knew the drill. By the time we were twelve, we had both learnt the route from town forwards and backwards. Down the path with the smiling face graffiti, cross the main road by the vets – look left, then right, then left again. Half-way down the hill nestles an ugly, heavy, overpowering church with a witty slogan outside. That night it was 'Don't go to waste. Let Jesus recycle you'. Carry on down the hill always giving a nod to the dead in the cemetery on your right. Not long now. Left at the kebab van and the welcoming light of bookies. But now you have a choice to make. You can stick to the main road; more people, traffic and stress, or you can take the backstreets home. A quicker route. A darker route. A scarier route.

Blue Beard passes on his way home.

Blue Beard   Good evening

Sisters (*nervously*)   Evening.

They all make the international sign for 'Help!' to suggest they are in trouble.

THE RETURN

Blue Beard *returns and sees the bin bags piled outside. He peeks inside them before knocking on the door.*

Blue Beard   I'm home.

Lucky *looks at her bloody Pierrot costume and in a panic rips it off. She stuffs it into a cupboard.*

Blue Beard   Let me in – you have my keys remember.

She runs to the door in her underwear, unlocks it and kisses him enthusiastically to cover her fear.

Well! This is a warm welcome. Did you miss me, my lucky charm?

Lucky   I did, husband. I did.

Blue Beard   You're undressed! Just how I like you. Let me take my coat off and you can tell me all your news.

Lucky   News?

Blue Beard   Yes. You must have lots to tell me.

Lucky   No news. I've just been waiting for you to come home.

Blue Beard   Is that right.

Lucky *kisses him again, trying to distract him.*

Lucky   Come to bed.

She tries to unbutton his shirt but he grabs her wrists.

Blue Beard   Not yet. I want to talk.

Lucky   OK. But it will be a very dull conversation.

Blue Beard   Don't play me.

Lucky   I'm not.

Blue Beard   Tell me.

Lucky   Tell you what?

He rolls up his sleeves.

Blue Beard   How tedious you are.

Lucky   Tedious?

Blue Beard   Alright.

He undoes his belt.

We'll do this your way. Just the way you like it.

Did you enjoy the house?

Lucky   Of course. I love it here. I love the space and the curtains and the kitchen and our bedroom . . .

She goes towards him, but he stops her.

Blue Beard   Can I have my keys back?

Lucky   Of course.

She finds the keys and hands them to him.

Here.

Blue Beard   I said – don't play me.

Lucky   I don't know what you mean.

He explodes with fury.

Blue Beard   The key.
The fucking key.
The key I told you . . .

Expressly . . .

Explicitly . . .

Not

To

Touch.

Lucky   I'm sorry.

Blue Beard   Where is it?

Lucky   I don't know.

He strikes the floor with his belt. **Lucky** *falls to the floor and flinches.*

Blue Beard   Where is it?

Lucky   I lost it.

Blue Beard *sits down to calm himself.* **Lucky** *stands.*

Blue Beard   Sit down.

Lucky   I want to . . .

Blue Beard   Sit down.

She does as she is told.

Perhaps you mislaid it when you were partying with your friends? When you were drinking my wine, eating my food and abusing my trust?

Lucky   I didn't abuse anything.

Blue Beard   Don't lie to me!

Blue Beard *starts to cry.* **Lucky** *stands to comfort him.*

Blue Beard   SIT DOWN!

She does. He weeps and writhes in torment.

I thought you were different.

Lucky   I am. I'm so sorry.

She starts to weep.

I love you.

Blue Beard   I don't believe you.

Mother Superior   The lovers sit in silence. Truth has fallen like snow.

The **Lost Sister** *starts her walk home.*

Without standing, **Lucky** *slowly makes her way towards* **Blue Beard**. *She touches him gently.*

Blue Beard *howls like a caged beast, leaps to his feet, grabs her by the hair and drags her outside where he throws her into the rubbish bags.*

Blue Beard   Tell me again that you didn't party.

Lucky   I was just . . .

Blue Beard   Just what? Behaving like the tramp you are?

He empties the contents of the bin bags all over and around her.

Where's my key?

He strikes the floor with his belt.

I said, where's my key?

She starts to look for it in the rubbish even though she knows it is not there. She is frantic. He goes inside and finds the key in the pool of water.

He calls gently.

Lucky?

Lucky   Yes?

Blue Beard   Come inside.

Lucky   But, I can't find it. I can't . . .

Blue Beard   Come inside. Do as you are told.

Lucky *comes inside to find* **Blue Beard** *holding the key.*

Blue Beard   You lied.

It was the only thing I asked of you, and still you lied.
EXPLAIN YOURSELF!

Lucky   I'm sorry. I didn't mean to lie. I love you. I'm so sorry. It was a mistake.

Blue Beard   Ah! A truth hidden amongst the trash and the falsehoods. It was a mistake. A big, big, big mistake.

THE SENTENCE

Mother Superior (*to the audience*)   You were fools to even think there was hope. Fools I tell you.

Blue Beard   You know what happens next, Lucky.
Lead the way.

Lucky *and* **Blue Beard** *walk through the house towards the door. The door of certain horror. They pass the open fridge but this time we see a skull on one of the shelves, the open wardrobe has hair hanging from a hanger and the magician's coffin has a floral tribute spelling 'LUCKY' on the top.*

Dead Assistant (*sings*)
Is your nose a-twitching, blossom?
Are your ears a-tuned to the threat?
Is your heart big enough to withstand the break?
Your chalk hands free of sweat?

Better wise up young one
Better get down and get low
No one is lucky forever
Beware the undertow.

What will you do when the luck runs out, dear?
What will you do when it fails?
Where are your dreams when the magic explodes?
Will you dig through the dirt with your nails?

FIGHT FOR SURVIVAL

When she reaches the red door, **Lucky** *turns sharply.*

Lucky   Wait.

Mother Superior   A rush of instincts race through her veins, a tsunami of spirit stirs.

Lucky   I don't want to die like this.
I know I am going to die, but not like this.

Mother Superior   If she can find a chink in his wall
Survival could be hers.

Lucky   Give me an hour. It is all I ask. Let me wash. Let me dress. Let me paint my lips as red as the love we felt when we met.

Blue Beard *holds her tear-stained, mascara-smudged face in his hands. Will he kiss her or break her neck? She whispers.*

Lucky   Let me die as the girl you married. I want you to remember me clean and pretty, grateful and lucky. Like I was when we met. No, when you found me.

Mother Superior   Look at him. Look at him – the narcissistic bastard.
Clever girl. You clever, clever girl.

Blue Beard   Very well. You have an hour.

Blue Beard *goes outside and smokes.* **Mother Superior** *joins him as the clock ticks.*

THE SUMMONING

Lucky *scrambles for the phone. Shaking and terrified, she dials.*

We see **Treasure** *and* **Trouble** *sat by the phone as it rings three times.*

Treasure *and* **Trouble**   One
Two
Three.

They look at each other. It has to be done.

THE UNTHINKABLE

Lucky *starts to plan her escape. She puts on a pair of trainers and unpacks his knives, swords and slicers.*

She waits for him, armed and ready to fight to the death. She is a harpy. A wolf. All femininity has left her and she is nothing but raw survival.

The hour is up and the alarm sounds.

THE REVEAL

Blue Beard *comes in. He too is changed. He is wild, almost animal. He laughs when he sees* **Lucky** *and they start the fight of their lives.*

Lucky *attacks him with his sword but he disarms her. They fight hand to hand, and he smashes her head into the piano before raising his sword for the final blow.*

FEMALE RAGE

There is a loud knock at the door and **Blue Beard** *stops. He places his hand over* **Lucky**'s *mouth.*

Blue Beard   Don't make a noise. They'll go away.

There is another loud knock.

What have you done?

There is another loud knock and he forces her to hide.

(*He shouts to the visitor.*) I'm coming. (*In a whisper.*) If it is your mother and sister I will kill them slowly and painfully and then I will kill you. Now be quiet.

He pulls himself together and goes to the door. He looks like a man again not a beast.

Who's there?

He sees a silhouette of his visitor. It is clearly a man in a coat and hat. **Blue Beard** *smiles and whispers to* **Lucky**.

Not the cavalry then. Looks like you're not so Lucky after all. Let me see what my visitor wants. Who knows, he might even want to join the fun . . .

Blue Beard *winks and opens the door.*

Hello, friend. What brings you to my door at this time of night?

The visitor   I was born to serve.

Blue Beard   To serve? To serve what?

The Visitor   To serve you justice.

The **Visitor** *takes off his hat to reveal that it is* **Treasure***, dressed head to toe in the Good Man's suit.* **Treasure** *throws a killer punch and* **Mother Superior** *blows her whistle.* **Trouble** *appears behind her, holding a bottle like a club.*

Blue Beard *turns back into his animal self and howls in rage.*

There is a fight to the death. **Blue Beard** *is dragged, cut, stabbed, routed and whipped. He is drugged and ridden like a horse, punched and kicked.*

The women work together to tie him to the knife-throwing target used in his act. They each throw a knife, but it is **Lucky** *who takes the final, deathly throw.*

THE KILL

Blue Beard *is dead. His limp body hangs from the knives that puncture his body. The women are covered head to foot in blood, weapons in hand. They look to the audience, avenging, heartbroken, desperate angels.*

Treasure*, a warrior, addresses the audience.*

Treasure   He called me Treasure, but it is I who has riches. My children. My brilliant, flawed, curious, trusting, vivid daughters. Who, like their father, I ask nothing of. Nothing except that they be happy and free . . . But happiness and freedom are not enough. I ask . . . No, I demand that they stay alive!

THE BURIAL

Mother Superior *talks to the audience as she buries the book, deep in the ground where it came from.*

*One by one, the **Sisters** come and join her.*

Mother Superior　No one wanted to touch the body, so we took him. The Fearful, Fucked and Furious took him. I think perhaps we wanted to be sure he was dead. And he was. We buried him in an unmarked grave and tramped the earth down on his vicious bones. But not before we shaved off his beard. His bastard blue beard. I put it on and have worn it ever since. I wear it as a memory of all the women torn down by men. I wear it as a promise to remember each and every life that has been cut short for male pleasure. And I wear it as a warning. A warning that we have had enough. Dear Gods, we've had enough.

*We see CCTV footage of the **Lost Sister** walking home. They are roads we walk every day. Roads we recognise.*

*The **Sisters** sing in sweet harmony as they watch the devastating footage.*

*We see the **Lost Sister** at a turning. She is deciding whether to take the main road or alleyway. She takes the alley. A man wearing a hoody appears behind her, we are relieved when he walks on.*

*After a few paces the man in the hoody stops and turns round. He walks back to the alley, checks left and right and follows the **Lost Sister**.*

*We see the hooded man exit the path alone. He looks straight into the camera then runs away. It is the same actor who plays **Blue Beard**.*

*The **Lost Brother** takes candles out of his sad rucksack and the **Sisters** light them to create a shrine.*

THE EPILOGUE

Mother Superior *takes off her wimple and lights a cigarette.*

Mother Superior　I never wanted to be a mum. I didn't not want to be one, I just never felt the burn like others around me did. But it's what you do and it's what I did. And kids are so bloody annoying. Messy. So bloody messy – always singing a song or playing with the dog instead of doing their homework or just being quiet. I wished my life away in a drudgery of odd socks, loud music, BO and cheap make up. I counted the hours until the door would shut, they were gone and I was finally alone. Peace.

She takes off her habit.

Rare, craved-for peace.

She takes off her beard. She is an ordinary woman like you or me.

Now there is no peace. I count backwards to the last time she left. I retrace time in case I find a gap in reality and can suck her back through that door. And if, if by some miracle she did walk through that door now, I'd bundle her up in black tee shirts and odd socks and hold on to her until she begged for freedom.

She howls in agony.

There's the burn. How can anything live in this unbearable heat?

She stops and feels her chest.

Wait. Something's in there. It is hatred. And it grows so big and strong that my heart can barely find the space to beat.

And that's OK with me.

She beats her chest.

Just give up and stop, you broken, burning, painful, pointless fucking bastard. Stop and let me go.

*She collapses in grief and the **Lost Brother** gathers her in his arms.*

Lost Brother   It's OK. It's OK.

Mother Superior   It's not OK. Leave me alone.

Lost Brother   I won't. Not this time.

Mother Superior *pushes free and stands alone. The* **Lost Brother** *speaks the question he has come to ask.*

Lost Brother   Can I walk you home?

Mother Superior   I am home.

Lost Brother   No, you are not, Mum.

Mother Superior *takes a breath but no words come out of her mouth.*

Treasure (*to the audience*)   And with that word. That small and massive word, 'Mum', her tears fell. The grief of centuries washed through the rage of today and something shifted.

Lost Brother   Please.

Trouble   And with that small and massive word, 'please' his tears fell.

The **Lost Brother** *weeps.*

Lost Brother   I'm so, so sorry.

Lucky   And with that small and massive word, 'sorry', the world's tears fell.

The **Lost Brother** *goes and gets his rucksack.*

Lost Brother   Come home, Mum.

This is no life. And you can't lock yourself away forever.

Mother Superior   I can and I will.

Lost Brother   I know she's gone but I'm still here. Let me walk you home.

Mother Superior   Enough. I said enough! You are messing with me and I don't appreciate this intervention. When and IF I leave I will walk home alone. I should be able to walk home alone.

Lost Brother   I know. But today. Now. Please let me. I didn't walk her home and . . . And I can't . . .

Mother Superior   I know.

Lost Brother   I'm so, so sorry.

Mother Superior   I can't.

The two sit. Stuck. Distant. Frozen in grief and fear.

The **Sisters** *take off their habits. Ordinary men and women all. They all sit. Lost. One holds the* **Lost Brother**'*s sign which still reads 'Help'.*

The **Lost Sister** *arrives.*

Lost Sister   What about me?

Mother Superior *and the* **Lost Brother** *see her.*

Lost Sister   I would like to go home.

Walk me home, Little Brother. Walk me home, Mum.

The **Mother Superior** *takes her daughter's hand. She turns and holds her hand out to the* **Lost Brother**.

Mother Superior   Come on lost boy. My own good man. Walk beside us.

The **Lost Brother** *takes her hand.*

They are joined by the rest of the sisters and brothers who take hands and walk each other home. Modern, good, damaged, hopeful people.

Mother Superior   We'll all walk each other home.

They walk through the audience and out onto the terrible and wonderful streets of now.

The End.